JAMES CONELY

# A GUIDE TO IMPROVISATION

An Introductory Handbook
for Church Organists

ABINGDON PRESS

NASHVILLE — NEW YORK

A GUIDE TO IMPROVISATION

*Copyright © 1975 by Abingdon Press*

All rights in this book are reserved.
No part of the book may be reproduced in any manner whatsoever without written permission of the publishers except brief quotations embodied in critical articles or reviews. For information address Abingdon Press, Nashville, Tennessee.

*Library of Congress Cataloging in Publication Data*
Conely, James.
  A guide to improvisation.

  Bibliography and discography: p.
  1. Improvisation (Music). 2. Organ—Instruction and study. I. Title.
  MT68.C654G8     786.7     74-26945

ISBN 0-687-16287-4

MANUFACTURED BY THE PARTHENON PRESS AT
NASHVILLE, TENNESSEE, UNITED STATES OF AMERICA

# FOREWORD

Most reference materials on organ improvisation presuppose that an organist is thoroughly familiar with harmony and counterpoint. For those who have acquired this training, fine. But what of those organists who, for one reason or another, have not had the opportunity for such detailed study? After all, there are a great number of organists of limited theoretical knowledge who must enter the church on Sunday morning and improvise during the service, regardless of former training and experience. It is to these organists that this book is directed.

Improvisation need not be complicated to be effective. But, on the other hand, "doodling" at the organ will not pass for interesting improvisation. How many of us have sat in church services listening to the organist nervously move from tonic to dominant and back again, waiting for the ushers to come forward with the offering plates? In such instances, silence would be less awkward.

All musicians draw on their own resources when they improvise. And so, in a very real sense, improvisation is a kind of "instant" composition based on various formulas already set down in the musician's mind. By using the simple step-by-step procedure described in this book, I feel that every organist will create a backlog of formulas upon which he can rely. The time will be well spent, and your congregation will thank you for it!

—David Bowman

# CONTENTS

Introduction.... 7

I  Rhythmic Pattern.... 9

II  Harmony.... 16

III  Melody.... 27

IV  Form.... 42

V  Registration.... 53

Selected References for Further Study.... 59

# INTRODUCTION

Simple improvisation can be easy if organists adopt specific plans and develop confidence in their ability to make music. Improvisation is not random or haphazard. Neither is it mysterious. Organists know what they are doing and should know it well. But even if their knowledge of techniques and theory is limited, they can improvise short pieces effectively if they believe in their ability to do so, are daring enough to try, and have planned their approaches very carefully. At the time of playing, therefore, they need only to improvise the notes; the style and structure have already been planned very carefully.

A number of methods can be used. The sequential one suggested here has five steps. It is not by any means the only one, but it is simple, direct, and useful for any improvisation regardless of length or difficulty, free-style or strict. In this order, the organist determines the:

a. rhythmic pattern
b. harmonic scheme and accompaniment
c. melodic pattern
d. form
e. registration

Then he or she plays.

This volume will describe each of these steps separately.

## CHAPTER I
## Rhythmic Pattern

In the sequential method rhythm is the unifying element for the whole improvisation. It is this element which makes an improvisation sound like a piece of music rather than a random search for notes. In fact, determining a specific rhythmic pattern will, in most cases, provide for an effective improvisation even if all the other elements are played randomly.

The rhythmic pattern, however, does not need to be complex or elaborate. Indeed, the improvisation may not even sound very rhythmical. It could be, for example, simply a slow, four-beat per measure pattern, but whatever it is, it should be specific and consistent throughout a short improvisation.

### Creating an Original Theme

Any rhythmic pattern is suitable for creating an original theme, but some are easier and sometimes more effective for service playing than others. When a pattern is chosen, it should be used either in the theme or in its accompaniment throughout a short improvisation. What follows is not a table of all possible rhythmic patterns, but rather a list of some suggested patterns that are useful for short improvisations:

# A GUIDE TO IMPROVISATION

(Sheet music exercises 7–30 for rhythmic improvisation in various time signatures: 4/4 for exercises 7–10, 3/4 for 11–20, 6/8 for 21–24, 5/4 for 25–27, 7/8 for 28–29, and 3+3+2/8 (Bartok) for 30.)

## RHYTHMIC PATTERN

Longer rhythmic patterns can be made simply by combining two or more of these patterns. However, long patterns are hard to remember throughout an improvisation, and they tend to be unnecessarily complicated. This increases the danger of a good improvisation deteriorating into meaningless sound.

The usefulness of these patterns can be demonstrated by choosing one and playing a scale in that pattern. Even without a carefully developed theme or accompaniment, the rhythm makes the scale acceptable as an improvisation in itself, depending on the stops, phrasing, and tempo chosen. For example:

## A GUIDE TO IMPROVISATION

The combinations of styles and rhythmic patterns are virtually endless. How they can be used either in accompaniment or melody will be shown in the next two chapters.

### Improvising on a Set Theme

An easy way to improvise or make variations on a set theme is to begin with the rhythm of the theme, changing the melody or other elements. This is easily done by reading the rhythm of the piece from the page during the improvisation. In many cases the rhythm is so characteristic that using it with almost any melodic or harmonic scheme can make a workable improvisation. This approach can be tested by isolating the rhythmic pattern of a hymn tune—for example, DIADEMATA ("Crown Him with Many Crowns")—and playing a scale in that pattern:

## RHYTHMIC PATTERN

This is an oversimplified variation, but it does make musical sense and therefore suggests that melodic schemes can be improvised almost at random and be effective if the rhythm is definite. Thus, the organist is free to adopt a variety of styles, thus avoiding the stilted style that often occurs in the common improvisations based on melody that simply change or add some notes here and there.

### Meter and Tempo

These two elements are close functions of rhythm. The simplest change of meter is from duple to triple meter and vice versa. Changing from duple to triple works very well in most cases, especially hymns, by dividing each duple-meter measure in half and then doubling the first beat of each new measure. Thus, a hymn tune such as NICAEA ("Holy, Holy, Holy") can be changed from:

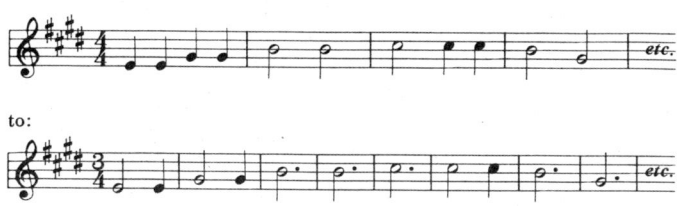

Similarly, triple-meter subjects can be changed to duple simply by doubling the first beat of each measure to two beats. Thus, a hymn tune such as MARYTON ("O Master Let Me Walk With Thee") can be changed from:

## A GUIDE TO IMPROVISATION

The style of the organist, the occasion for improvising, and the theme used all determine the appropriateness and use of the change in meter. All of this depends on the purpose for the improvisation, which must be carefully considered in determining any style and technique.

The same consideration is true for tempo. In most cases tempo determines itself by the nature of the improvisation, but sometimes the organist chooses a particular tempo to create a certain effect. For example, the rhythmic pattern |$\frac{3}{4}$ ♩ ♩ ♩ | ♩ ♩ ‖ can be very effective for quiet meditation when played slowly; the same pattern played faster suggests a grand march, especially if played *marcato*. Choosing tempo depends on the use for the improvisation.

### Summary

Effective improvisations are easiest when they are based on specific and constant rhythmic patterns such as those listed in this chapter. Having determined rhythm, an organist is then ready to continue building the improvisation by determining an effective harmonic scheme and accompaniment pattern.

### Suggestions for Practice

1. Choose any rhythmic pattern from those listed on pages 9, 10 and play a scale in that rhythm up and down one

## RHYTHMIC PATTERN

octave. Repeat the pattern as often as necessary, but don't play any notes twice in succession. Adjust the notes at the end so that you stop on the key note. Follow the examples on page 11.

2. Choose another rhythmic pattern, and play the same scale in that pattern, ending again on the key note.

3. Create your own two-measure rhythmic pattern, and play a scale in that pattern.

4. Open a hymnal to your favorite hymn. Follow the rhythmic pattern of the melody precisely, and play a scale in that pattern.

5. Change the meter of the same hymn (for example, duple to triple meter), and play the notes of the melody in the new meter.

6. Create a new style for the same hymn by changing the tempo and using the meter chosen in step 5 above.

## CHAPTER II
# Harmony

The most successful improvisations, and the easiest, are the ones which create their own harmonic patterns. This can be done in a variety of ways, three of which are explained here.

### Progressions by Thirds

Because the sound and pattern of thirds are so deeply ingrained in Western civilization, this chord construction is instinctive. Thus for most people, it is the easiest construction to improvise. However, because it seems so natural, it can easily lead to unimaginative improvisations that sound either like the organist doesn't really know what to do or that he never knows anything *new* to do.

One way to be creative with thirds is to start with a simple, basic triad—let's say C, E, G. Now instead of using it in the familiar I, IV, V (C, F, G) chord progression, let the notes establish their own progression. Perhaps the chords would then be C major, E major, G major, and progress precisely in that way. When combined with a rhythmic pattern chosen from chapter 1, this new progression could comprise a complete short improvisation:

Rhythmic pattern 14:
Trpt. fanfare

# HARMONY

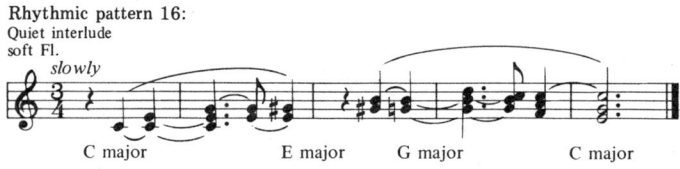

Another progression of chords might be scalewise up a third, then down a third, and back to the key note:

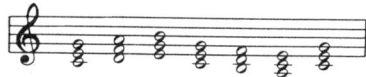

With a specific rhythmic pattern, a short improvisation using this progression might then be:

A third very easy technique is to select any note, playing an improvisation using only chords with that note in them—chords that are again constructed from triads. If the note were A-flat, then perhaps the improvisation would be:

Various other techniques are possible, but these three may be the easiest to master at first. Others may be suggested by other kinds of chord structure, such as the one discussed next.

**Progressions by Fourths**

Twentieth-century composers have reminded us that harmonic structure need not be based exclusively on thirds. Fourths are just as easy to construct and can provide a refreshing contrast to the traditional sound. This becomes a very useful procedure, therefore, for easy improvisation. It consists simply of having intervals of a fourth between notes of a chord instead of intervals of a third.

Thus, the familiar triad C, E, G:

may become C, F, B:

Observe also that the inversion of intervals of the fourth produces intervals of the fifth:

So it happens that these intervals can be effectively combined. When pairs of them are used together, but with the

# HARMONY

two pairs separated by a third, the result can be a very smooth, reflective improvisation. The chord structure would then be like this:

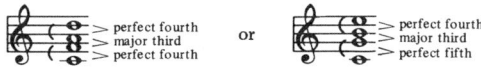

Improvising becomes simply a matter of applying this structure to harmonize a melody. For example:

FOUNDATION ("How Firm a Foundation")
Ged. 8′

## A GUIDE TO IMPROVISATION

Although many serious musicians may scoff at this conclusion, the simple truth is that the organist can usually shape his or her hands in the configuration of these combined fourths and fifths and produce a beautiful improvisation on a melody with no greater study of harmony.

### Tone Clusters

To be even more creative, an organist can harmonize by tone clusters. This need not be an unpleasant sound, nor does it need to sound *avant garde*. For example, select the softest stop—perhaps erzahler or flauto dolce with celeste—and play the following:

Rhythmic pattern 25:

With a definite rhythmic pattern, these improvisations can be entirely spontaneous and yet create the impression that they are very carefully prepared "pieces," especially if used as accompaniment for flute or soft reed solos. For example:

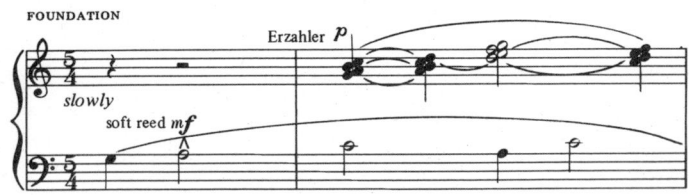

## HARMONY

Sometimes clusters can be used within octaves to create a mass of sound for ceremonial improvisations, as in a processional:

The harmonics present in certain organ stops make it possible to use clusters easily. Organists do not need to be unnecessarily bound to traditional theory of harmony. They need only to experiment with various patterns to discover that many creative and effective sounds can be produced on their instruments.

### Progressions for Harmony

Many harmonic progressions can be studied and used for improvisations. Organists can adopt traditional patterns such as the familiar I, IV, V, I sequence:

Or I, VI, II, V, I:

## A GUIDE TO IMPROVISATION

These patterns are common and useful, and organists can easily create a short improvisation by assigning each chord to a specified number of measures, playing them in a particular rhythmic pattern, and providing a simple scale-like melody.

However, in most cases such improvisations end up sounding alike, and worse, they too frequently become uninspired, self-conscious time fillers to take up space during a service while waiting for something else to happen. To make *music* should be the goal. And so organists need to have alternate techniques at their ready disposal.

Adopting other uses of these progressions will usually prevent trite improvisations. Particularly useful are parallel motion, contrary motion, ascending soprano descant, and descending bass line. These techniques are commonly used in music and are easy to improvise by establishing the line deliberately and consistently:

**parallel motion**—All lines move together in the same direction:

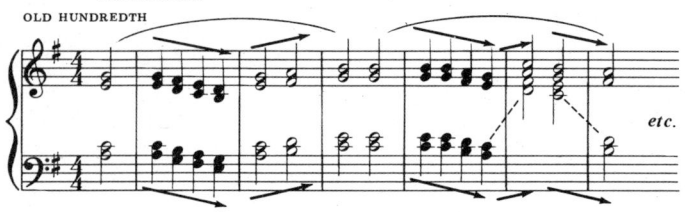

**contrary motion**—The soprano and bass lines move in opposite directions:

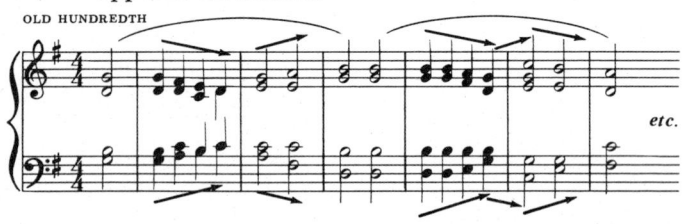

## HARMONY

**ascending soprano line**—The soprano line moves up in a specified time and range (usually a fifth or octave) with all chords or other melodic lines accompanying that movement but not necessarily parallel to it:

**descending bass line**—The bass line moves down in a specified time and range with all chords or other melodic lines based on that movement:

**constant line**—The entire improvisation is based on a single note which is either sustained or repeated but never changed. In effect the organist tries to find a number of chords that can effectively use that note. Then, he or she plays them in a specific rhythmic pattern, as in the last example in the section called "Progressions by Thirds" earlier in this chapter.

The key to the success of all of these approaches is the consistent pattern they provide for an improvisation. Any other pattern can therefore be used equally as effectively providing it is precise and is maintained throughout. This

## A GUIDE TO IMPROVISATION

must be regarded as the essential difference between an improvisation that is musical and one that merely sounds like a frantic, aimless search for notes.

### Accompaniment Figures

Chord patterns can be played in many ways for accompaniment, including all the traditional styles such as Alberti bass and ostinato:

These are all good, but the person who has never improvised before or who has done so ineffectively wants to find a pattern that can be used for *any* melodic figure.
One such pattern might be this:

This pattern is most effective for very short improvisations intended to set atmospheres of awe, introspection, or contemplation. It can be used regardless of the key, range, or style of the melody. For example:

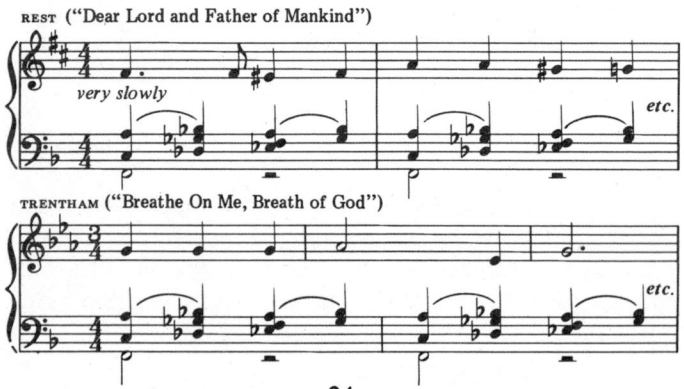

## HARMONY

Other similar patterns can easily be found. Organists must be cautioned not to use this or any single pattern for all improvisations. Once their confidence in improvising is established, they need to avoid being trite or repetitious.

### Summary

With a definite and consistent rhythmic pattern, harmonic progressions can become complete improvisations in themselves. The procedure suggested here calls for determining a specific chord structure by thirds, fourths, or clusters, then adopting a harmonic progression for these chords which might be parallel, contrary, ascending soprano descant, descending bass line, or constant line. Accompaniment figures can then be chosen, one of which is suggested here for use with any melodic line regardless of key. This prepares organists to add their own improvised melodies.

### Suggestions for Practice

1. Select a basic triad in any key and select any progression for it that is based on the notes in the triad. Now choose a rhythmic pattern from pages 9, 10 and play the progression in that pattern as a short improvisation. Follow the examples on pages 16, 17.
2. Find five different triadic chords in which one note is the same in all of them. Play the chords in one of the rhythmic patterns chosen from pages 9, 10 ending on the tonic chord. Follow the example on page 17, 18.
3. Choose a short hymn such as WOODWORTH ("Just As I Am"), ST. ANNE ("O God, Our Help in Ages Past"), or LET US BREAK BREAD TOGETHER. Harmonize the melody by shaping your hands in the configuration of fourths

# A GUIDE TO IMPROVISATION

and/or fifths in the manner shown in the example on page 19. Keep the phrasing very smooth and play *legato* throughout.

4. Choose your softest stop with either celeste or tremulant. Play a tone cluster in a specific rhythmic pattern slowly and very *legato*. Add a solo hymn melody on another manual similar to the example on page 20.

5. Play a trumpet fanfare by playing a short C-major scale melody in octaves in a specific rhythm and with three-note clusters on white keys only in the middle of the octaves. Follow the example on page 21.

6. Play your favorite hymn with its own rhythm and harmonic structure but with the melody and bass lines following these contours (refer to pages 22, 23 for examples):

   a. parallel motion
   b. contrary motion
   c. ascending soprano descant
   d. descending bass line

7. Play the melody of your favorite hymn with the following accompaniment. Do not transpose the melody; play it as written regardless of its key or meter.

## CHAPTER III
# Melody

From a listener's viewpoint, the most clearly recognizable element of any piece of music is the melody. It is also the easiest element to create. If the rhythm and harmony are carefully thought out and performed deliberately, virtually any melody or melodic fragment will work effectively in an improvisation. Special consideration is therefore given here to certain kinds of melody.

### Melodies Derived from Harmony

In sequential improvisation harmony is determined before melody. Thus, the chords and their progressions can be used themselves to improvise an appropriate melody. This is easiest to do by selecting a sequence of notes found in the chords, playing them within a limited range—usually an octave—and perhaps adding passing tones for a smoother melodic line. This can be demonstrated using the familiar I, IV, V⁷ harmonic progression:

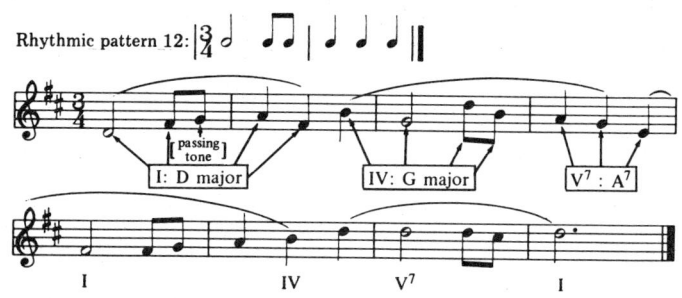

## A GUIDE TO IMPROVISATION

Assuming the organist is much more creative and has improvised a different harmonic progression, he or she may produce much more interesting and imaginative melodies. For example, suppose the organist is basing the improvisation on chords constructed of fourths progressing in contrary motion. The melody and its accompaniment might then be something like this:

This same approach can be used for any other combination of chord structure and progression by playing notes of the chords individually and adding other appropriate notes.

### Scale Melodies

Using scale melodies assumes first of all that a key or key center has been determined. Then notes are chosen within that key for both the melody and harmony. The melody usually moves stepwise. In other words, the melody is derived without accidentals and usually without skips between notes. Three kinds of scales seem to provide the easiest sources of original, improvised melodies: diatonic, modal, and whole tone.

Diatonic has become the most established of all scale patterns in Western civilization in the past three hundred years. It is therefore the most instinctively natural one for short improvisations. Using it consists simply of choosing any specific diatonic scale and selecting notes for the melody exclusively from that scale. This selection can be a deliberate and studied choice of notes, but it works just

## MELODY

as effectively at random if the rhythmic pattern and harmonic progression are definite and consistent. The examples given in the introductory section of this chapter follow this technique precisely.

The seven so-called church modes provide a number of possibilities for very interesting and beautiful improvised melodies. The technique for creating melodies by these scales is the same one just described for diatonic scales; the only difference is that the source of the melody is modal rather than diatonic.

The easiest way to determine modal scales is to play all white keys from any note on the keyboard to the same note in the next higher or lower octave. Thus, C to C produces the familiar diatonic scale, otherwise called the *hypolydian* mode. D to D produces the *dorian* mode, E to E produces the *phrygian* mode, and so on. Hence, the seven modes are:

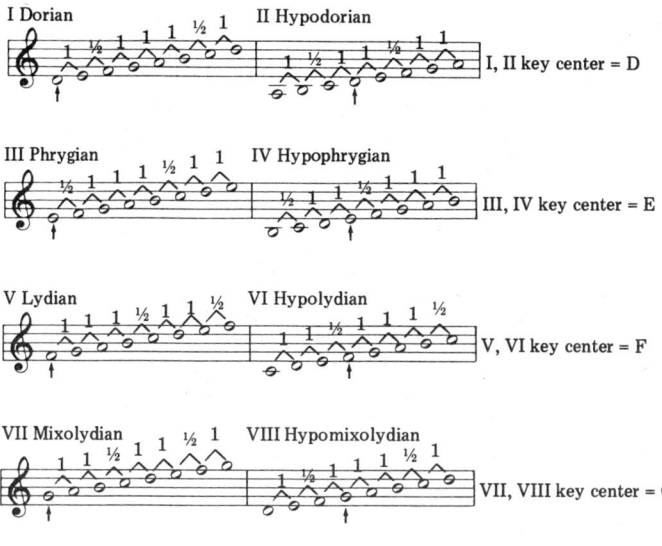

## A GUIDE TO IMPROVISATION

These modes, of course, may be transposed to any range, and they then use black keys just as the diatonic scale does when it is played in any other key besides C. The intervals between scale notes remain the same regardless of the key note. The organist can therefore choose a mode and play it in the range desired.

Modal transposition then becomes an interesting possibility in itself:

OLD HUNDREDTH (diatonic)

Mode II: Hypodorian beginning on G

Hence, OLD HUNDREDTH in Mode II:

Mode IV: Hypophrygian beginning on G

Hence, OLD HUNDREDTH in Mode IV:

## MELODY

Unlike diatonic and modal scales, there are only two whole tone scales regardless of what note they begin with:

One clear advantage of using a whole tone scale is that the listener does not hear any one note as being a key center. Thus, he does not expect any particular harmonic or melodic progression. Furthermore, the aesthetic and psychological quality of a whole tone scale is in itself intriguing. The simplest and most random improvisation can therefore sound like an inspired, carefully composed piece of music. Thus, the organist need not be concerned with trying to create a perfect melody—it will create itself automatically if its rhythm and harmony are definite.

To demonstrate this, here is a short list of random numbers taken from an authorized source of such numbers:
49487 52802 28667 62058 87822 14704 18519*

*Reprinted by permission from *A Million Random Digits with 100,000 Normal Deviates,* The Free Press of Glencoe, Illinois, copyright 1955 by the Rand Corporation.

## A GUIDE TO IMPROVISATION

Letting each number correspond to a whole tone scale note—

—and using two of the rhythmic patterns listed in chapter 1, the following melody results:

## MELODY

The point of this demonstration is not to suggest using a table of random numbers for improvising. Certainly the improvisation ought to be more musical than that. Rather, the point is that improvising whole tone melodies is so easy that the organist can direct attention to the creation of music rather than the selection of notes.

### Hymn Tunes

Hymns are very useful for improvisations, especially when the organist wants to use a melody the congregation will recognize. One clear advantage is that the organist may follow a line of printed music. Furthermore, when an improvisation is used to maintain continuity in a service, it can easily be based on a hymn just sung or about to be sung.

For example, suppose the choir sings an Introit that uses a characteristic rhythmic pattern and is followed immediately by a hymn. If the organist begins the introduction to the hymn by playing the Introit rhythm to accompany the hymn tune, the mood is sustained and the effect for the congregation increases.

The easiest way to create variations on the melody is to use passing tones where they can occur naturally in the hymn. For example:

# A GUIDE TO IMPROVISATION

A more interesting approach is to use a melodic fragment of the hymn tune as the basic theme for the whole improvisation. Here the concern is not so much in hearing the tune as it is in hearing what music may be suggested by a part of the tune. A characteristic fragment may then be extended into a fully developed melody of its own:

## MELODY

The listeners feel the spirit and thought of a particular hymn but avoid focusing on the hymn itself. This may occur, for example, when communion elements are being distributed. Here whatever music is used should enhance the service rather than call direct attention to the music.

In addition to changing harmony, using passing tones, and extending a melodic fragment, the organist may use any of the traditional techniques of thematic development. Three of these are especially easy to improvise: augmentation, diminution, inversion.

For example, if the theme is—

—then the following techniques could result:

augmentation:

diminution:

inversion:

The organist who seriously wants to develop ideas on how to vary hymn tunes would do well to analyze carefully the chorale preludes of J. S. Bach. These are, after all, arrangements of hymns. In them can be seen that constant rhythmic patterns and well-defined harmonizing schemes provide for natural melodic variations. Furthermore, within certain ones are implied suggestions the organist can use in performing the chorale preludes themselves. Thus, they can be used as an exercise to develop improvising skills.

To do this, examine a chorale prelude such as "I Call to Thee, Lord Jesus Christ," noting that Bach did not specify melodic ornaments (or variations) to use in the second half of the piece. Then determine how the ornaments are used in the first half and apply them in the second half. Bach in effect has begun the improvisation; now the organist can continue. The result might be this:

# MELODY

# A GUIDE TO IMPROVISATION

## Phrasing

It is important to realize that improvising notes for a melody will not in itself create good music. All of the expressive techniques must be used and used well. Of these the most critical is phrasing. More than anything else this will determine whether a melody sounds random or organized, erratic or meaningful, verbose or cogent, monotonous or vibrant. Proper phrasing makes the difference without changing any note.

Consider the following examples:

The only difference here is the way the notes of the melodic line are phrased, yet the two examples create very different melodies. The organist must therefore think carefully about the musical idea to be communicated and phrase it so that it is expressed most effectively.

## Summary

Creating melodies may well be the easiest step of improvisation. It can be done by using notes of the harmonic pattern, various scale patterns, or hymn tunes. Whatever the source, the organist can improvise musically if careful to phrase meaningfully and appropriately for the musical idea to be communicated. Having done so, the next consideration is establishing an overall form or structure, which is considered in the next step of sequential improvisation.

## MELODY

### Suggestions for Practice

1. Play the same improvisations you created for the first two practice exercises on page 25. Draw a melody from the notes of each chord as you play it adding, if you wish, passing tones.

2. Choose notes at random from any major scale, and play them unaccompanied in one of the rhythmic patterns on pages 9, 10 ending on the key note. Play this new melody again and harmonize it.

3. Choose three of the church modes listed on page 29, and create melodies from them in the same manner as for the diatonic scale in exercise 2 above.

4. Play the melody of a short choral response, such as a two- or three-fold "Amen," in the hypodorian mode. Determine the scale intervals from the list on page 29. Select one other mode (except hypolydian) and play the same melody in that mode.

5. Create a melody from a whole tone scale with a specific rhythmic pattern in the same way that you did for diatonic and modal scales. Harmonize the melody from the same whole tone scale.

6. Improvise on a hymn such as "Come Thou Almighty King" using passing tones in the melody and by expanding a melodic fragment of it in the manner of the example on page 34.

7. Play the same hymn three times—first by augmentation, then by diminution, and finally by inversion. Use passing tones in the bass line where appropriate, but otherwise keep the harmony essentially as written. Follow the examples on pages 35, 36.

8. Play "I Call to Thee, Lord Jesus Christ" by J. S. Bach using the ornaments written out on page 37. Study the derivations of the ornaments used after measure 5. Now see if you can apply the same kind of analysis to the

## A GUIDE TO IMPROVISATION

Telemann chorale below, adding ornamentation to the melody in the style of J. S. Bach.

## MELODY

9. Using ideas suggested by Bach's ornamentation, improvise on the melody of a hymn in a similar way but in your own style: embellish the line, add scale fragments on long notes, try long and short trills on the next to last note of each phrase, etc. For purposes of practice, try anything that will elaborate on the melody. Avoid being critical or in any way judging the quality of your improvisation. Try a number of different improvisations on the same hymn to increase your ability to do it naturally, easily, and automatically.

CHAPTER  IV

Form

An improvisation must have some sort of clearly identifiable form, or it will invariably sound rambling and incoherent. No concerned musician wants that. Regardless of the length of the spontaneous composition, an organist should aim for structure so that listeners have a sense of an idea being introduced, developed to a logical climax, and ending. Furthermore, the organist will find it is much easier to improvise when musical ideas are in a specific framework, because the framework itself will suggest what to do.

Improvising form can be very sophisticated, but it doesn't necessarily have to be. There are organists who readily create double fugues, but even they find that occasions requiring such an improvisation are rare or nonexistent. In other words, when they improvise a double fugue, it is because they can and want to—not because they have to. In any case, it is usually best for the beginner to start with a very simple idea and create for it a very simple and short form. This will build both skill and confidence. It is also much more useful for most improvisations.

The first principle to realize is that length of the theme is of no concern whatever. The object of form is not to make the melody long enough to last through the time required of the improvisation. Rather, the object of form is to develop the theme logically regardless of its length or complexity.

# FORM

## Extended A and ABA

For the reason just stated, a good basic pattern is one we may call "extended A" form. In this, the theme or motif is stated at the start, is developed by restatement in different positions or keys, is briefly referred to in its original position at the end, and the piece stops. It is thus a kind of through-composed piece that can be done easily and simply in an improvisation as short as one minute. It need not be any more involved to be developed satisfactorily:

Rhythmic pattern 14:
Harmonic scheme: primarily open fifths
Melody: Mode II - Hypodorian
Form: extended "A"

## A GUIDE TO IMPROVISATION

Other examples of such pieces can be found in my *Eighteen Short Pieces and Modulations,* especially the pieces in C major, E-flat major, A minor, and B-flat major.

If the middle section of this form is developed somewhat more, then the result becomes in effect an ABA form. No more skill or theory is required to achieve this. The three-part ABA form is satisfying aesthetically because it has the effect of beginning, departure, and return.

The easiest way to develop this form is to create two short "extended A" pieces. Then play them in sequence, with the first one repeated after the second one.

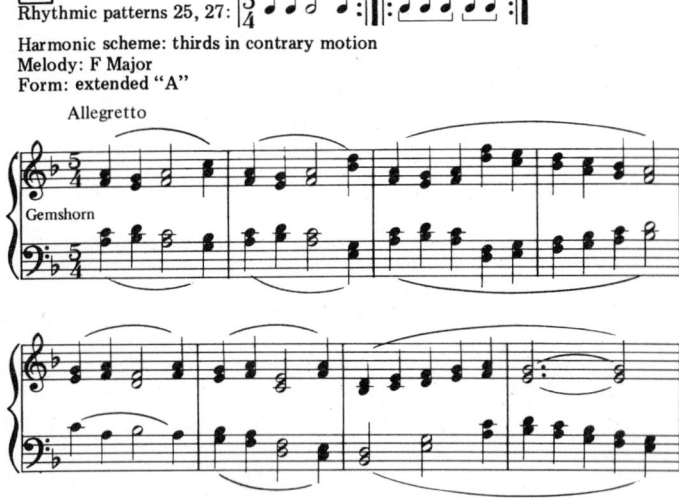

# FORM

## A GUIDE TO IMPROVISATION

If each theme is well organized and systematically improvised, then a competent and satisfactory three-minute improvisation can be virtually guaranteed. The organist is then well on the way to improvising on his own—creating ideas and patterns of development at the time of performance.

### Improvised Hymns

Sometimes a hymn-like improvisation is desired. This, too, is easy if the organist adopts the style and structure of a particular hymn. Essentially this is a matter of setting the rhythmic pattern and chord structure according to common hymns, using techniques of the first two steps of this book. Normally, this will be either $\frac{3}{4}$ or $\frac{4}{4}$ meter with four-part triadic chord structure.

For example, LANCASHIRE ("Lead On, O King Eternal") is an AB form in which A consists of four measures that are repeated, and B consists of an eight-measure extension of A. Hence, an improvised hymn tune based on this structure might be as follows:

# FORM

NICAEA ("Holy, Holy, Holy") is in AA′ form in which A consists of an eight-measure theme, and AA′ consists of a repetition of A with a variation of the ending. An improvisation on this structure might be this:

# A GUIDE TO IMPROVISATION

Forms of other hymns are equally as easy to recognize. Once recognized they are then almost as easy to improvise.

## Simple Polyphony

The creative organist will also want to try polyphonic improvisations. This requires more control and a clearer conception of the idea to be developed. However, it can be done with relative ease by starting with a two-voice piece in freestyle.

Again, the best approach is to use a very short extended A form for each voice. The theme itself will be easiest to improvise the first time if it is drawn from a whole tone scale, as described in chapter 3. The reason for this is that the notes in each voice will harmonize naturally with each other. The organist is therefore free to develop each line at will without feeling constrained to "find" certain notes that will sound right together.

With this basic material the improvisation can start with one voice playing a portion of the theme alone. Then

## FORM

as it continues, the second voice can enter playing the same melody on a different pitch. For example:

## A GUIDE TO IMPROVISATION

Here, then, is the beginning of a fugue-like composition which can be developed as long or as intricately as the organist wishes. Now, however, it must be realized that this is no more than a start—an exercise, if you will, to gain a feel and confidence in improvising polyphony. To use it well requires study in developing the musical idea according to sound principles, both structurally and melodically. The organist should therefore accept this as a challenge rather than discouragement. After the initial

# FORM

introduction to improvising gained by this point the organist will surely find his or her interest whetted to study it more.

## Summary

A number of forms are possible, and the organist is well advised to identify them specifically and use them deliberately in improvising. This need not be a detailed study nor need it lead to complex compositions. But it will guarantee a musical result that is much more satisfying than beginning with an idea with no direction for its development.

## Suggestions for Practice

1. Extend the following theme another eight measures and end it by leading into a repetition of the first two measures (extended A form), but stop on an F major chord.

Rhythmic pattern 2: |4/4 d ♩♩ | ♩♩ d :||
Harmonic scheme: fourths, fifths in parallel motion
Melody: F major
Form: extended "A," 16 measures

# A GUIDE TO IMPROVISATION

2. Create your own extended A form in F major, F minor, or D minor.

3. Create an ABA form by using the two themes you created for steps 1 and 2 above, as in the example on pages 44-46.

4. Analyze the structure of a short hymn tune, such as AMAZING GRACE, noting in particular its chord progression. Now improvise a new hymn tune by creating a new melody for the same rhythm and chord progression.

5. Create a free polyphonic improvisation first by playing your own extended A melody in a whole tone scale. Remember to base it on a specific rhythmic pattern. Now accompany it with a single line of notes imitating the melody at a different pitch. Avoid parallel movement between the two lines.

CHAPTER V

# Registration

At this point the organist has a fairly simple step to perform but one that ought to be accomplished with the same care as the preceding steps: selecting the stops to use. Improvisers too often are content with a bland registration, such as Salicional played very softly so that the congregation can't tell what the organist is really doing. Perhaps complete silence would be better in such cases.

However, the registration can be musically interesting itself even if it is very quiet. It can also help determine the style and development of the improvisation. Depending on the purpose of the improvisation and on the resources of the individual organ, a number of different kinds of combinations are possible. What follows is a list of some possible registrations for various uses.

### Meditation

Use any quiet flute or string stop, with or without tremulant. For example:

   a. Dulciana, Erzahler, or soft flute with Celeste
   b. Gemshorn
   c. Kleine Gedackt
   d. Quintadena

### Chorale or Hymn

Use a rather broad sound, even if quiet. Have enough brilliance in the sound so that the harmonization is clear.

# A GUIDE TO IMPROVISATION

For example:
   a. Flutes 8' and either 4' or 2'
   b. Gemshorn 8' and Spitz Principal 4'
   c. Principals 8', 4', and III-rank Mixture
   d. Principal 8', Octave 4', Twelfth 2⅔', Doublette 2'
   e. Principal 8', IV-rank Mixture, Fagott 16', Clarion 4'

## Solo

Be creative. Use stops with unique characteristics that are interesting because of their particular quality of sound, especially orchestral solo reeds like oboe, clarinet, English horn, bassoon. For variety try using tremulant with a quiet string or flute accompaniment but not with the solo. Experiment to find new combinations that are unique and perhaps otherwise unexpected. For example:

   a. Chimney Flute 8' and Larigot 1⅓'
   b. Gedackt or Quintadena 16', Gamba and Gamba Celeste 8', Vox Humana, French Horn, Flute 4', Tremulant
   c. Gemshorn 8', Nazard 2⅔'. Flute 2', Tierce 1⅗'
   d. Gedackt 8', Flute 2'
   e. Rohrflote 8', Flutes 4' and 1⅓'
   f. Fagott 16' (played one octave higher), tremulant
   g. Koppelflote 4' (played one octave lower)
   h. Pedal: Flute 4' or Schalmei 4'

## Polyphony

The stops need to be bright and clear. Ordinarily if all voices of the polyphony are played on the same keyboard,

## REGISTRATION

use a combination of flute or principal stops rather than reed or string stops. For example:

a. Flutes 8' and 2'
b. Flutes 8', 4', and 1'
c. Principals 8', 4', and 2'
d. Bourdon 8' and II-rank Sesquialtera

If the voices are played on separate keyboards, use distinctive and different sounds for contrast. For example:

| If Manual I is: | then Manual II might be: |
|---|---|
| Krummhorn | Gedackt<br>*or* Gemshorn<br>*but probably not*<br>Oboe<br>*or* Schalmei |
| Flutes 8', 2' | Krummhorn<br>*or* Quintadena<br>*but probably not*<br>Gedackt 8', 2'<br>*or* Gemshorn 8', 2' |
| Gedackt 8', III-rank Zimbel | Trompette<br>*or* Krummhorn<br>*but probably not*<br>Flute 8', III-rank Scharf<br>*or* Copula 8', Cornet |

# A GUIDE TO IMPROVISATION

## Ceremonial

Use a bright, full combination but be careful not to make it too loud. Ceremonial improvisations may take several minutes, as in a processional, and if the registration borders on fortissimo for too long, it becomes difficult to maintain musical direction for the theme. It then rapidly loses its interest. Judicious use of reeds, mixtures, and mutation stops can create the impression of a full, massive sound without being overpowering. For example:

a. Principal 8', Octave 4', IV-rank Mixture
b. Flute 8', Trompette 8', III-rank Mixture
c. Gemshorn 8', Principal 4', III-rank Mixture, Fagott 16'
d. Gamba 8', Twelfth 2⅔', Clarion 4'

With any of these registrations as a foundation, other stops can be added as desired during the improvisation, thus providing musical interest in the sound itself. Of course, much depends on the size of both the organ and the room in deciding how many stops should be used as the foundation.

## Summary

Registration is basically a matter of using taste, imagination, and personal judgment in selecting stops that make the best combination of sounds. Inasmuch as all organs are different, the organist needs to determine what stops sound best on his own organ, but even on the smallest organ he can find new combinations that are interesting and useful. Such creativity is what sets apart a good improvisation from one that is simply adequate.

# REGISTRATION

## Suggestions for Practice

1. Go back to the improvisations you created for the first four steps and choose stops for each one from the following categories:

   a. meditation (page 53)
   b. chorale or hymn (page 53)
   c. solo (page 54)
   d. polyphony (page 54)
   e. ceremonial (page 56)

2. Play each improvisation again but change either the stops within a category above or change the category. See how many different styles you can create for the same improvisation by changing the registration, tempo, and phrasing.

3. Improvise a three-minute piece on your own by this sequence:

   a. First choose a definite rhythmic pattern.
   b. Then determine a specific harmonic scheme and accompaniment.
   c. Create a melody out of the harmony or scale.
   d. Fix an ABA or other form in mind for the improvisation.
   e. Select stops according to the style and purpose you have in mind.

4. Improvise at every opportunity to build your confidence and skill. Listen analytically as you play, and enjoy the music you make. Then continue your study by (a) observing closely good church organists in recital or service playing, (b) studying references such as those listed in the section on "References for Further Study," and (c) working with a skilled teacher.

# Selected References for Further Study

## Articles

All of the articles listed below will be found in *Music,* the magazine of the American Guild of Organists and the Royal Canadian College of Organists.

Bowman, David. "Dupre's Master Improvisation." Oct., 1973, p. 22; Nov., 1973, p. 34. A careful analysis of one of the great improvisations of the twentieth century.

Getz, Pierce. "An Introduction to Organ Mixtures." Nov., 1971, p. 44. An easy-to-understand explanation of the function of mixtures and how to use them.

Phillips, Nancy L. "Exams for Fun?" Jan., 1972, p. 18. The section on improvisation and modulation gives some particularly practical and easy approaches with illustrations useful for service playing.

Suitor, M. Lee. "Techniques for Accompanying." Dec., 1972, p. 28. Includes adapting piano scores, arpeggiated chords, repeated chords, and other techniques.

Watters, Clarence. "Improvisation." May, 1973, p. 27; June, 1973, p. 24. An excellent introduction to advanced study; assumes basic knowledge of form, harmony, and counterpoint.

## Books

Dupré, Marcel. *Cours Complet D'Improvisation a L'Orgue.* Paris: Editions Musicales Alphonse Leduc. The definitive text for thorough study of organ improvisation.

## A GUIDE TO IMPROVISATION

Enright, Richard. *Introduction to Organ Playing* (APM-366). Nashville: Abingdon Press, 1964. Progressive lessons from simplest manual exercises to three and four-part counterpoint.

Gleason, Harold. *Method of Organ Playing.* New York: Appleton-Century-Crofts, 1962. The modern standard text for organ instruction in general.

Goode, Jack C. *Pipe Organ Registration.* Nashville: Abingdon Press, 1964. Step-by-step directions for using and understanding the organ as an instrument. Includes stops, combinations, history of the organ, and a dictionary of organ stops.

Hilty, Everitt Jay. *Principles of Organ Playing.* Boulder: Pruett Publishing Co., 1971. A practical and useful text with numerous music examples and exercises.

Johnson, David N. *Instruction Book for Beginning Organists.* Minneapolis: Augsburg, 1973. Includes free harmonization for hymns and improvisation as well as general instruction.

Konowitz, Bert. *Music Improvisation as a Classroom Method.* Port Washington: Alfred Music Company, 1973. Although intended for high school classes in general school music, Dr. Konowitz's method is so clear and logical that many useful approaches to improvising can be learned from this book.

Krapf, Gerhard. *Organ Improvisation.* Minneapolis: Augsburg, 1973. Practical study in formal improvisation; includes chorale fughetta, hymn preludes, hymn index, many music examples; assumes a working knowledge of harmony and counterpoint.

SELECTED REFERENCES FOR

Walters, Samuel. *Basic Principles of Service Playing.* Nashville: Abingdon Press, 1963. A basic and practical guide for all aspects of service playing.

## Music

Bach, Johann Sebastian. *The Liturgical Year (Orgelbüchlein).* Edited by Albert Riemenschneider. Oliver Ditson 77123-137. Baroque master variations of hymn tunes with notes for study and performance.

Baumgartner, H. Leroy. *Variations on Hymn Tunes.* APM-564. Abingdon Press. Easy arrangements that demonstrate ways to improvise on hymn tunes.

Bielawa, Herbert. *Four Preludes on Hymns of the Church.* APM-543. Abingdon Press. Moderately difficult.

Buxtehude, Dietrich. *Choral Transcriptions.* Edwin F. Kalmus 3279, 3280. Urtext edition.

Conely, James. *Eighteen Short Pieces and Modulations.* Belwin-Mills F. E. 10016. Demonstrates some short forms and includes an index of modulations from 18 keys to all other keys and brief illustrations of some uses of modulations for hymns.

———. *Organ Music for Celebration and Praise.* APS 6003. Summy-Birchard, 1974. A collection of pieces by various composers; the ones by Herman Strategier, Marcel Dupre, and Flor Peeters are particularly good illustrations of ways to develop short pieces.

Copley, R. Evan. *Three Chorale Preludes.* APM-253. Abingdon Press. Moderately easy.

Curry, W. Lawrence. *Fifteen Hymn-tune Preludes for Organ.* APM-449. Abingdon Press. Moderately easy.

# A GUIDE TO IMPROVISATION

Diercks, John. *Six Sacred Compositions for Organ.* APM-425. Abingdon Press. Moderately difficult.

Johnson, David N. *Music for Worship for Manuals.* Augsburg 11-9297. Easy arrangements of hymns; useful for study and performance.

Karg-Elert, Sigfried. *Interludes in Various Keys.* Hinrichsen (C. F. Peters Corp., sole agents), Edition No. 93. Short improvisatory pieces in various styles.

Lapo, Cecil E. *Four Organ Preludes on Chorale Tunes.* APM-225. Abingdon Press. Moderately easy.

Marshall, Jane. *Fifteen Harmonizations on Hymn Tunes.* APM-231. Abingdon Press. Easy. Different harmonic treatment of familiar hymn tunes.

Nalle, Billy. *Alle was du bist* (Jerome Kern: "All the Things You Are"). World Library 0-3001. A chance to improvise eight measures within the piece; clever, fun, and different.

Peeters, Flor. *Thirty-Five Miniatures and Other Pieces for Organ,* compiled by James Conely. APS 6034. Summy-Birchard. Short, easy pieces mostly for manuals alone demonstrating effective improvisatory styles.

Pfautsch, Lloyd. *Three Organ Preludes on Hymn Tunes.* APM-352. Abingdon Press. Moderate difficulty.

Rohlig, Harald. *Fifty-five Hymn Intonations.* APM-256. Abingdon Press. Easy. New ways to introduce familiar hymns for congregational singing.

———. *Thirty New Settings of Familiar Hymn Tunes.* APM-286. Abingdon Press. Moderately easy.

## SELECTED REFERENCES FOR

Telemann, Georg Phillipp. *Twelve Easy Choral Preludes.* Edwin F. Kalmus 4005. Urtext edition. Very useful Baroque pieces for both study and service playing.

Viderø, Finn. *Twenty-One Hymn Intonations.* Concordia 97-5004. Hymn variations with an index for six hymnals.

*Voluntaries for the Christian Year, Vol. I.* APM-526. Abingdon Press. Moderate. Hymn tune preludes by various composers.

*Voluntaries for the Christian Year, Vol. II.* APM-914. Abingdon Press. Moderate. Hymn tune preludes by various composers.

Walter, Samuel. *Nine Compositions for Organ.* APM-426. Abingdon Press. Moderate. Mildly contemporary treatment of hymn tunes.

———. *Six Hymn-Tune Preludes.* APM-257. Abingdon Press. Moderately easy.

Withrow, Scott S. *Twelve Hymn Accompaniments with Descants.* APM-384. Abingdon Press. Moderately easy.

Young, Gordon. *Organ Music.* Broadman Press. Simple settings of hymns.

### Records

Brittenham, Robert. *Organ Improvisations.* Disc available from the artist: 84 Hillis Terrace, Poughkeepsie, N. Y. 12603. Improvisations recorded during Lutheran services that can suggest many ideas to other organists.

Cochereau, Pierre. *L'Extraordinaire Pierre Cochereau aux grandes Orgues de Notre Dame de Paris.* Philips 6521008. The great French organist improvises on "Alouette" and other French songs.

## A GUIDE TO IMPROVISATION

———. *Treize Improvisations sur les Versets de Vêpres.* Philips 835732. Improvisations that make *music* for services.

Erwin, Lee. *Sound of Silents.* Angel S-36073. Recorded on the Washington, D.C., Fox-Capitol Wurlitzer, now in a private home. One of the original master theater organists plays his improvisations in the grand style; excellent for study and listening enjoyment.

Hancock, Gerre. *Improvisation.* Disc available from the Music Secretary, Saint Thomas Church, 1 West 53rd Street, New York, N. Y. 10019. A master improviser demonstrates the potential variety of music in hymns; an excellent illustration.

Johnson, David N. *Beginning Improvisations and Compositions of D. N. Johnson.* Wicks Organ Company 832 W-3352 (Highland, Illinois 62249). Illustrations of a fine teacher at work; a good companion to his textbooks.

Nalle, Billy. *Big Bold and Billy!* Project 3#PR-5053-SD (Total Sound, Inc., 1270 Avenue of Americas, New York, N. Y. 10020). Recorded on the Brooklyn Paramount Wurlitzer now installed at Long Island University. Theater organ is instructive, especially as an example of the effectiveness of variety in tonal color. This recording has been reported to have been used in certain college courses in classical improvisation.

Tournemire, Charles. *Four Improvisations Reconstructed by Maurice Duruflé* (with four pieces of Louis Vierne); Maurice Duruflé and Marie-Madeleine Duruflé-Chevalier organists. Musical Heritage Society MHS 1016. Magnificent compositions reconstructed from recordings of an improvising genius.

786.7
C75G

294949

**Johnson Free Public Library**

Hackensack, New Jersey